B♭ TRUMPET

MW00991341

FILM FAVORITES

Solos and Band Arrangements Correlated with Essential Elements® Band Method

Arranged by
MICHAEL SWEENEY, JOHN MOSS and PAUL LAVENDER

Welcome to ESSENTIAL ELEMENTS FILM FAVORITES! The arrangements in this versatile book can be used either in a full concert band setting or as solos for individual instruments. The SOLO pages appear at the beginning of the book, followed by the BAND ARRANGEMENT pages. The supplemental CD recording or PIANO ACCOMPANIMENT book may be used as an accompaniment for solo performance.

ISBN 978-0-634-08698-4

HAL•LEONARD® CORPORATION

7777 W. Bluemound Rd. P.O. Box 13819 Milwaukee, WI 53213

00860149

From Walt Disney Pictures' **PIRATES OF THE CARIBBEAN: THE CURSE OF THE BLACK PEARL**

PIRATES OF THE CARIBBEAN

(A medley including: The Medallion Calls • The Black Pearl)

B♭ TRUMPET
Solo

Music by KLAUS BADELT
Arranged by MICHAEL SWEENEY

00860149

From the Paramount and Twentieth Century Fox Motion Picture TITANIC

MY HEART WILL GO ON

(Love Theme From 'Titanic')

B♭ TRUMPET
Solo

Music by JAMES HORNER
Lyric by WILL JENNINGS
Arranged by JOHN MOSS

From THE MUPPET MOVIE

THE RAINBOW CONNECTION

B♭ TRUMPET
Solo

Words and Music by
PAUL WILLIAMS and KENNETH L. ASCHER
Arranged by PAUL LAVENDER

From THE LORD OF THE RINGS: THE FELLOWSHIP OF THE RING

MAY IT BE

B♭ TRUMPET
Solo

Words and Music by EITHNE NI BHRAONAIN,
NICKY RYAN and ROMA RYAN
Arranged by JOHN MOSS

From Walt Disney Pictures' TARZAN™

YOU'LL BE IN MY HEART

B♭ TRUMPET
Solo

Words and Music by
PHIL COLLINS
Arranged by MICHAEL SWEENEY

00860149

From the Motion Picture SHREK 2

ACCIDENTALLY IN LOVE

B♭ TRUMPET
Solo

Words and Music by
ADAM F. DURITZ
Arranged by MICHAEL SWEENEY

Featured in the Motion Picture 2001: A SPACE ODYSSEY

ALSO SPRACH ZARATHUSTRA

B♭ TRUMPET
Solo

By RICHARD STRAUSS
Arranged by MICHAEL SWEENEY

00860149

From the Paramount Motion Picture MISSION: IMPOSSIBLE

MISSION: IMPOSSIBLE THEME

B♭ TRUMPET
Solo

By LALO SCHIFRIN
Arranged by MICHAEL SWEENEY

From SHREK

MUSIC FROM SHREK

(A medley including: Fairytale Opening • Ride The Dragon)

B♭ TRUMPET
Solo

Music by JOHN POWELL
and HARRY GREGSON-WILLIAMS
Arranged by JOHN MOSS

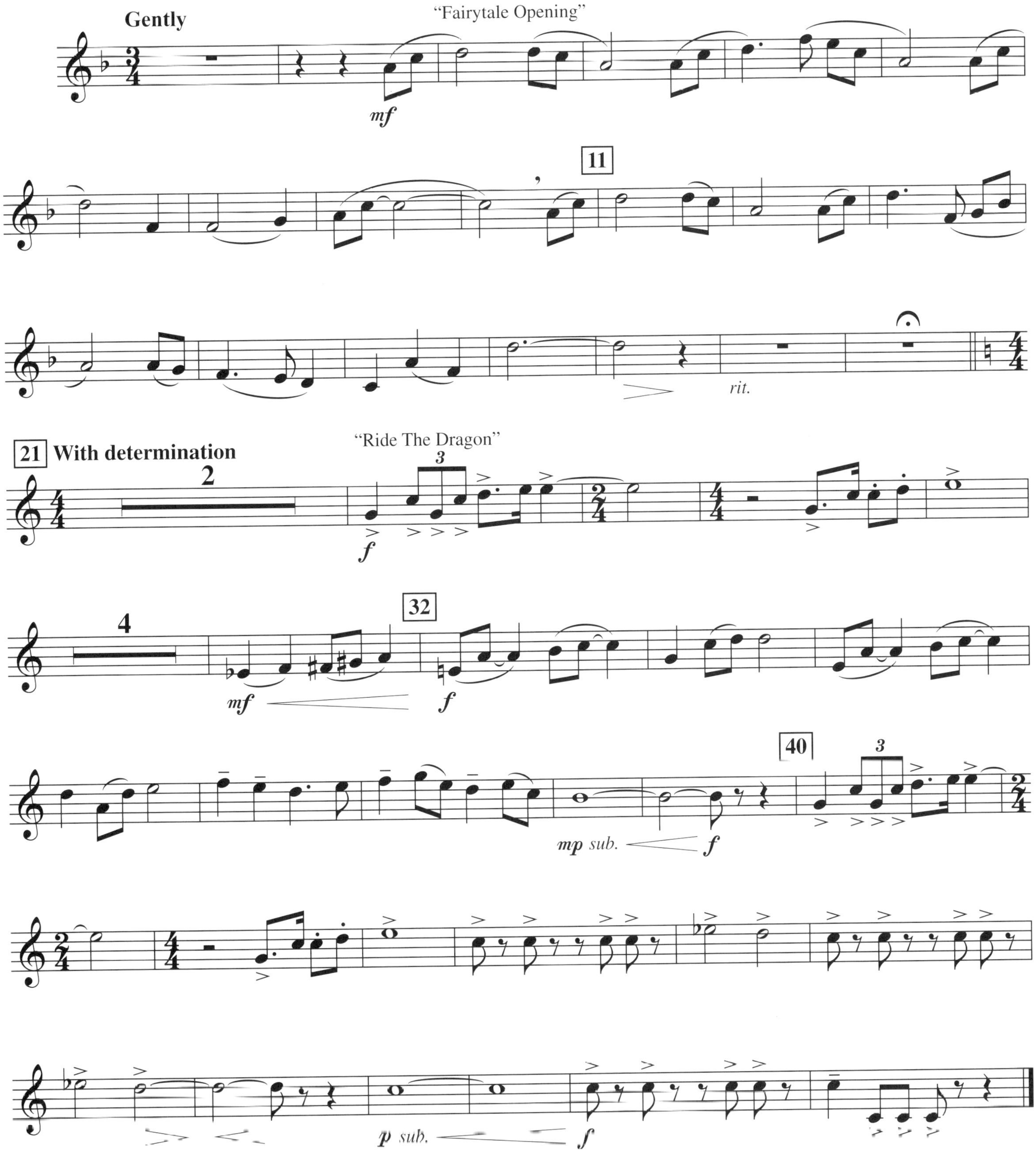

00860149

From the TriStar Motion Picture THE MASK OF ZORRO

ZORRO'S THEME

B♭ TRUMPET
Solo

Composed by
JAMES HORNER
Arranged by JOHN MOSS

From Walt Disney Pictures' PIRATES OF THE CARIBBEAN: THE CURSE OF THE BLACK PEARL

PIRATES OF THE CARIBBEAN

(A medley including: The Medallion Calls • The Black Pearl)

B♭ TRUMPET
Band Arrangement

Music by KLAUS BADELT
Arranged by MICHAEL SWEENEY

From the Paramount and Twentieth Century Fox Motion Picture TITANIC

MY HEART WILL GO ON

(Love Theme From 'Titanic')

B♭ TRUMPET
Band Arrangement

Music by JAMES HORNER
Lyric by WILL JENNINGS
Arranged by JOHN MOSS

From THE MUPPET MOVIE

THE RAINBOW CONNECTION

B♭ TRUMPET
Band Arrangement

Words and Music by
PAUL WILLIAMS and KENNETH L. ASCHER
Arranged by PAUL LAVENDER

00860149

From THE LORD OF THE RINGS: THE FELLOWSHIP OF THE RING

MAY IT BE

B♭ TRUMPET
Band Arrangement

Words and Music by EITHNE NI BHRAONAIN,
NICKY RYAN and ROMA RYAN
Arranged by JOHN MOSS

From Walt Disney Pictures' TARZAN™

YOU'LL BE IN MY HEART

B♭ TRUMPET
Band Arrangement

Words and Music by
PHIL COLLINS
Arranged by MICHAEL SWEENEY

From the Motion Picture SHREK 2

ACCIDENTALLY IN LOVE

B♭ TRUMPET
Band Arrangement

Words and Music by
ADAM F. DURITZ
Arranged by MICHAEL SWEENEY

00860149

Featured in the Motion Picture 2001: A SPACE ODYSSEY

ALSO SPRACH ZARATHUSTRA

B♭ TRUMPET
Band Arrangement

By RICHARD STRAUSS
Arranged by MICHAEL SWEENEY

From the Paramount Motion Picture MISSION: IMPOSSIBLE

MISSION: IMPOSSIBLE THEME

B♭ TRUMPET
Band Arrangement

By LALO SCHIFRIN
Arranged by MICHAEL SWEENEY

From SHREK

MUSIC FROM SHREK

(A medley including: Fairytale Opening • Ride The Dragon)

B♭ TRUMPET
Band Arrangement

Music by JOHN POWELL and HARRY GREGSON-WILLIAMS
Arranged by JOHN MOSS

00860149

From the TriStar Motion Picture THE MASK OF ZORRO

ZORRO'S THEME

B♭ TRUMPET
Band Arrangement

Composed by JAMES HORNER
Arranged by JOHN MOSS

00860149

MORE FAVORITES FROM ESSENTIAL ELEMENTS

These superb collections feature favorite songs that students can play as they progress through their band method books. Each song is arranged to be played by either a full band or by individual soloists, with optional accompaniment on CD.

Each song appears twice in the book, featuring:

- Solo instrument version
- Band arrangement for full band or ensembles
- Pop-style accompaniment CD included with conductor's score
- Accompaniment CD available separately
- Piano accompaniment book that is compatible with recorded backgrounds

Prices:

- Conductor Books.. $24.95
- Instrument Books.. $4.95
- Piano Accompaniment Books................................ $9.95
- Accompaniment CDs....................................... $12.95

Instrument books for each collection feature separate books for the following: Flute, Oboe, Bassoon, B♭ Clarinet, E♭ Alto Clarinet, B♭ Bass Clarinet, E♭ Alto Saxophone, B♭ Tenor Saxophone, E♭ Baritone Saxophone, B♭ Trumpet, F Horn, Trombone, Baritone B.C., Baritone T.C., Tuba, Percussion, and Keyboard Percussion.

CHRISTMAS FAVORITES

Arranged by Michael Sweeney

Songs include:
The Christmas Song
(Chestnuts Roasting on an Open Fire)
Frosty the Snow Man
A Holly Jolly Christmas
Jingle-Bell Rock
Let It Snow! Let It Snow! Let It Snow!
Rockin' Around the Christmas Tree
Rudolph, the Red-Nosed Reindeer.

MOVIE FAVORITES

Arranged by Michael Sweeney

Includes themes from:
An American Tail
Back to the Future
Chariots of Fire
Apollo 13
E.T.
Forrest Gump
Dances with Wolves
Jurassic Park
The Man from Snowy River
Raiders of the Lost Ark
Star Trek

BROADWAY FAVORITES

Arranged by Michael Sweeney

Songs include:
Beauty and the Beast
Tomorrow
Cabaret
Edelweiss
Don't Cry for Me Argentina
Get Me to the Church on Time
I Dreamed a Dream
Go Go Go Joseph
Memory
The Phantom of the Opera
Seventy Six Trombones.

PATRIOTIC FAVORITES

Arranged by Michael Sweeney

Songs include:
America, the Beautiful
Armed Forces Salute
Battle Hymn of the Republic
God Bless America
Hymn to the Fallen
My Country, 'Tis of Thee (America)
The Patriot
The Star Spangled Banner
Stars and Stripes Forever
This Is My Country
Yankee Doodle/Yankee Dookle Boy

FOR MORE INFORMATION, SEE YOUR LOCAL MUSIC DEALER,
OR WRITE TO:

HAL•LEONARD® CORPORATION
7777 W. BLUEMOUND RD. P.O. BOX 13819 MILWAUKEE, WI 53213

Visit Hal Leonard Online at **www.halleonard.com**

Prices, contents, and availability subject to change without notice. Some products may not be available outside the U.S.A.

0902